GIRAFFES

Sandie Lee Books

Giraffes

The Giraffe is the tallest land mammal on earth and the biggest animal that is considered a ruminant. Like a cow, the giraffe chews its cud and also has four compartments in its stomach. There are 9 subspecies of the giraffe. The West African giraffe and the Ugandan giraffe are both on the endangered list. This is due to their habitat loss and to poaching. You can see giraffes at zoos and in some protected parks.

Where in the World?

Did you know that giraffes live in Africa? They like to roam the savannahs, open woodlands and also forests that are near a body of water. Mother giraffes with their young will stay out in the open. This makes it easier to see predators and to protect the baby giraffe.

The Name of a Giraffe

Did you know the scientific name of the giraffe is, camelopardalis? Because of the hump on its back and its spotted fur, early peoples called the giraffe a "camel-leopard." So this is how it got its name, because the giraffe looks like a cross between a camel and a leopard.

The Body of a Giraffe

Did you know each giraffe has a unique spotted pattern? Just like human fingerprints, the giraffe's spots are all different from one another. The giraffe has a long neck with the same number of vertebrates as we do. Plus, it has long legs and 2 small horns on top of its head.

The Size of the Giraffe

Did you know the male giraffe can be 18 feet tall? A female giraffe measures around 14 feet tall and the baby is already 6 feet tall when it is born. Even the giraffe's tongue is long. It can measure up to 20 inches. Its tongue is also prehensile - like a monkey's tail.

The Heart of a Giraffe

Did you know the giraffe has a huge heart? The human heart is only about the size of our fist. The giraffe's heart measures about 2 feet long. It can weigh up to a whopping 25 pounds! Since the giraffe is so big, it takes a big muscle to pump blood throughout its huge body!

What a Giraffe Eats

Did you know the giraffe likes vegetables? The giraffe eats mainly leaves, buds and twigs of the acacia and mimosa trees. This animal can pack away up to 75 pounds of food every day. Considering it only eats a few leaves at a time, this is a lot of munching and crunching. In fact, the giraffe spends most of its time eating.

The Giraffe's Special Ability

Did you know the giraffe is a fast runner? The giraffe can run at speeds of up to 37 miles-per-hour. It can gallop for long distances at 31 miles-per-hour. When the giraffe is walking, it moves its legs on one side on its body, then the legs on the other side of its body.

The Giraffe's Defense

Did you know the giraffe uses its neck to fight for a mate? When two males battle, they will swing their long necks at each other. This is called 'necking.' The giraffes try to hit each other with their horns and to knock the other one away. The strongest one wins.

The Giraffe as Prey

Did you know the giraffe can be prey? Baby giraffes can fall prey to hyenas and lions. The adult giraffes are rarely hunted by lions unless they are old or injured. One kick from a healthy giraffe is sure to send a smaller animal flying. Giraffes are also hunted by man for trophies.

Giraffe Talk

Did you know giraffes can communicate? Even though giraffes are quiet animals most of the time, they still make some sounds. Moms will make a hissing or low growling sound when her young are being naughty. Male giraffes will make a noise like a cough when they are trying to attract a mate.

The Giraffe Mom

Did you know the male giraffe flirts with the female? Male giraffes will graze beside a female and also wrap his neck around hers. After the female becomes pregnant, she will carry the baby giraffe for 14 months. That's a long time - humans carry their young for 9 months!

The Baby Giraffe

Did you know the baby giraffe has a long fall when it is born? Giraffes give birth to their young standing up. The baby is born head first and falls to the ground from about 6 feet up. This does not hurt the young. In fact, the fall surprises the baby giraffe into taking its first breath.

Giraffes at Rest and Play

Did you know the giraffe only sleeps about 5 minutes at a time? Even though the giraffe is a tall animal it has to stay alert. It does this by sleeping only about 20 minutes a day. The rest of its time is spent grazing and galloping along their home lands.

Life of a Giraffe

Did you know the giraffe can live to be around 25 years old? Even though the habitat of the giraffe is shrinking, they still manage to survive in the wild. Giraffes in captivity (like zoos or animal preserves) can live to be a lot older. This is because the giraffe is protected from predators.

Quiz

Question 1: What was the giraffe called by the native people?

Answer 1: A camel-leopard.

Question 2: How big is a baby giraffe when it is born?

Answer 2: A baby giraffe can be 6 feet tall at birth

Question 3: How big is an adult giraffe's heart?

Answer 3: 2 feet long and weighs 25 pounds

Question 4: What is the giraffe's special ability?

Answer 4: It is a fast runner - 31 miles-per-hour

Question 5: How long does a giraffe sleep per day?

Answer 5: 5 minutes at a time for a total of about 20 minutes each day

Thank you for checking out another addition from Sandie Lee Books! Make sure to check out Amazon.com for many other great titles.